Life and Times in Bedford, Virginia

TIM ZIMMERMAN

Fulton Books
Meadville, PA

Published by Fulton Books 2024

ISBN 979-8-89221-181-9 (paperback)
ISBN 979-8-89221-182-6 (digital)

Printed in the United States of America

I was born on East Main Street, a small town, in 1959, when things were simpler. My dad was a merchant marine, and my mom was a bookkeeper. I had very loving parents. I was the only child, not spoiled but was provided for. I had a lot of good days with my dad and mom. When my dad was gone to sea, Mrs. Fogle, a lady next door, watched me after school. They were good country folks. He was a good cook, my mom not so much. I remember one time there was lightning outside, Dad and Mom said to come inside. Hardheaded me would not listen until lightning came through a rake and shocked me. Then I listened!

One time I cut my finger on a knife. I told Dad a rosebush cut it, but he knew what had happened. I remember when I was three years old, my grandmother was supposed to be watching me. I snuck out the back door while my dad was coming in the front door from painting the roof. It was about forty feet up. I climbed the ladder looking for my dad if he was going to spank me. He told me I was a teenager. He was glad to get me down safe and sound. When my dad was home from the sea, my mom would head out. I would tell her that my stomach was hurting so that I could hang out with my dad. We would go to Lynchburg, Virginia, in his 1962 VW. We would be home by lunch so that my mom would not know. We had lot of fun. I just wanted to spend time with my dad. He was a good man and father.

My mom wasn't much of a cook. My dad cooked all the time when he was home. But when Dad was coming home, I tightened up. I remembered times were simple. My mom took me to church, where I learned about God. I loved it. She was a good, religious woman. My first car was a Mustang. It had a slipping transmission, and on the right side, it was wiped out. My parents got it for me for $600. That was a lot of money back then. I loved the car. We didn't have a lot of money, but my parents were good-hearted people.

I didn't know what a shower was until I was eighteen years old. I thought I was rich. I started my first job at fourteen. I delivered groceries after school for fifty cents an hour back in 1975. When I was grown up, me and another boy down the street would play on East Main Street. We had a lot of fun. I remember my dad was gone one time, and my mom bought me a new pair of blue suede boots. We went down to the railroad tracks, and I messed them up. Mom wasn't too happy.

I started my job at trailways at $8.95/hour. More money than I had ever made. I've been blessed. I have raised two kids who were not mine, a boy one month old and a girl thirteen months old. I love them to this day. They are in their forties now. I still talk to them. They both live in Georgia. My parents loved them very much. My dad passed away in 2005 and my mom in 2009.

We grew up with a johnny house in the back on East Main Street. Some had to wash in pans. I took a bath in a clawfoot tub until the age of eighteen. Then we had a shower when I left home. Also back in 1960, we had grapevines behind us. I remember one time my dad was trying to make wine brandy one night, and the wine blew up in the crock. Scared us to death. We had a lot of good times in the sixties. As time went on, we approached the seventies. Times were still simple, but then I was becoming a teenager. I remember my thirteenth birthday in the living room of mom and dads. I had some friends over. I thought I was big at that time in life. Also remember going to dances at the Bedford army. At sixteen, I had a birthday party at one part of the army.

We used to ride my mini bike around the army that I got at age 9. My dad got it for me at Roses. I was thrilled that Christmas. I still have it to this day. We also had a little dog named Blue. My dad loved that little dog. He lived nineteen years. Also coming up, Mom got me a duck at Easter. It grew up fast. Dad and Mom finally had to give it to Mrs. Fogle. She took it to the country.

As a child, we went to Florida to see my dad's mom every summer for a week. We always went to Gatorland. As a kid, I always wanted a baby alligator and monkey. I never got either. Maybe it was for the best as I look back. My first guitar was brought at a Body Camp store. I was so excited. My uncle, Mom's brother, lived in Body Camp. He had a big white horse. We would go down to the farm when Dad was gone every other weekend. I had a horse named Trigger that I rode down the farm. We also went down the road to Loyd Ayers, where we would enter horse shows. We got a lot of ribbons, which was fun. As the late seventies came, I went back to Florida to live. I worked at Disney World for one year. That was great, and I had a lot of fun. When I returned back to Bedford, that's when I met the kids' mom. Robert, the boy, was in a laundry basket. I fell in love and got married. I went to work.

By this time, we were in 1982. Life was simple. We lived in Deans Trailer Park—$35 a month lot to rent. The kids had a lot of fun growing up. While I was living in the trailer park, trailways went out of business. I went across the street and got a job with a linen company driving. I was there five years. It was a lot of hard work and long days, but good times. At twenty-seven years old, I thought maybe I had better settle down and put a roof over our heads. I bought three acres of land and put a trailer on it during the eighties and early nineties. The kids and myself had good times. In 1992, the lady and the kids moved to Georgia. That is where her family lived. I put a double wide on land. I knew a guy named Jack Johnson who lived close by. He was a good man.

I got a job with RUS, a linen company. I loved route work. It soon became Cintas in 2002. I stayed at my job for twenty years. Left in 2009 when my mom passed away. Finally in the late eighties, I bought three acres of land in the country. Put a home on the land. As time went on, in the nineties, I got divorced. I soon met a wonderful lady in 1997. Her dad passed away in 1999. He was a very good man. We married in 1999. Her mom wanted someone to be close to her, so we put a double wide on three acres close to her on the farm. Times were happy for over twenty years. Like I said, my mom and dad had passed away. I was asked to resign at Cintas after being there thirty years. But life went on.

I took care of my mom when she was sick. I sure miss her. She worked at Sam Moores in the office for thirty-five years. Dad had seventeen years at sea. They were good parents. Mom took good care of me when Dad was gone. Made sure I was doing the right thing. I remember one time my mom could not figure out why I was so sick. She took me to four doctors. Then she took me to a specialist in Roanoke, Virginia. He told her to get me home and me under thick covers. Chicken pox came out of my body. That's what was wrong with me. My dad went out in a blizzard in his VW to get me some medicine. He was there for me always. I had a very good raising and moral values. Where has this world gone to! I am not perfect by all means. I have always been a hard worker and a caring person. Not everyone had a good childhood. I have nothing to complain about even though at times, life has been a struggle. I went to church with my mom when I was young. I didn't have a lot of money, but I do things from my heart, and that means more too.

My wife had a seizure April 1, 2019, after her mom passed. She had a lot of stress on her and lacked sleep. She's doing good and hasn't had any more, thank God. So much to be thankful for. We have a grandson. His name is Noah. He's a lot of fun and brings joy. My wife babysat him when he was only six weeks old, and he's ten now. We get him from school, and we both love him dearly. Lots of good times. We moved from our home of twenty years in 2002. We have a stick-built home now. I had a friend who helped me a lot. His name was Mike Sloan. We went to basketball games and did things together a lot. He passed away, and I sure do miss him. I met him at RUS.

I met a man from overseas in 1997. I worked for him part time. He was a good man. He had a heart attack in 2013. I miss him also. God has been with me through the years of heartache. I also had another friend, played with him on East Main Street. He passed away in 2013. My other childhood friend passed away several years ago. We would leave lunch in seventh grade and go to Tyler White Store. Boy, I miss those days. We grew up together. He was always there for me.

I cut grass in the sixties and seventies for a lady down the street. That house that my mom and dad owned is still there. The house I lived in was built in 1849.

While living on the farm, Noah, our grandson, would come over and we would ride the four-wheelers together. We would walk the farm and do all kinds of things. We had good times on the farm. We still have fun together. We play ball, and whatever he wants to do, we try to do it. He doesn't understand that I am sixty-three years old, but I do what I can with him. He keeps me young. I bought him a 1966 VW. Going to save it for him when he starts driving. Going to teach him how to drive a straight drive. Also, I got him a guitar. Hopefully he will take lessons and learn how to play it.

When I was two years old, my dad and mom had a bunch of rabbits which multiplied quickly. We also had a weeping willow tree in our yard. It finally fell. We also had a cigar tree which stayed around for many years. When I was young, our yard went way out, then the process came along in the early seventies. The city wanted to make four lanes on East Main Street. It look a lot of our front yard. Growing up in the early seventies, we had a Bedford County Lake and a drive-in. We all hung out, and there was always something to do for us all back then. I remember at Christmas, we had a Sears store and a Sears catalog to look through and pick out something. We would also go to the Roanoke, Virginia, to see Santa come in on a rooftop at the Sears on Williamson Road. Snows were deep in the late sixties. Good for the sleigh riding, which we all did and had a blast. A lot has changed since then in Bedford. We have the D-Day Memorial for World War II veterans. We also have what used to be a Greens Drug Store. It is now a Bedford Boys, where you can come in and see war items and pictures of the Bedford Boys.

Bedford, Virginia, is a very good place to live. We have the beautiful Peaks of Otter, Blue Ridge Parkway. We also have Smith Mountain Lake, which is just an awesome five hundred miles of shoreline. When the kids were small, we would go to the parkway to see animals. Bedford has a lot of history. If you want a good place for you and the kids, Bedford is a nice little town. I have nothing to complain about. We have a lot of beauty here in Virginia. As a little boy, I thought there would be more to do here, but there is less to do now. But as an older person, it is just right. Not a lot of opportunities for young people.

By this time, you know that I was raised in Bedford, Virginia, for twenty-three years, since 1997. I have a wonderful life and a wonderful wife. I love my church. As a child, I played softball and also dug first dirt for the church when it was going to be built.

My dad told me growing up that they had two movie theaters. As a kid, we would go camping in the parkway on Jennings Creek and fish. What good times we had. My mom's mom lived with us for a long time. Mrs. Fogle was a wonderful lady. She was great with animals, and she had a lot of birds all the time.

Always loved the springtime here in Virginia. Winters are very mild. I love Bedford. It is a good place to live. I've been very blessed. A lot of people have moved here since 1959. Don't blame them for moving into a nice little town away from all the traffic. I love to get out and talk with people. You learn a lot.

It's still a pretty simple life here. God is great. I miss the simple times for sure. A lot of good people have moved here to this small town. I love talking to people, hearing their stories. I always have loved springtime. It's beautiful here in the spring.

I have met a lot of good people since I left my job in 2009. I have been to California. I went there in 2016 for six months. Nice people there, but it's still not like my hometown here in Bedford. I still do route work to this day in Bedford. All in all, it's a great place to be.

My dad was gone from six to ten months. He was a merchant marine. I would talk to him, and I missed him very much. I remember when we would put him on the Greyhound bus, I would cry and cry. I knew that I would not see him for a long time. But I knew that between my mom and the lady next door, that I would be taken care of. My mom was a very loving and godly person, so I knew that she would see that I was taken care of.

Life in Bedford, Virginia, has been good. I worked two jobs for twenty-five years. One job was a four-days-a-week job, and the other was an extra job whenever I wanted to work. Life sure has been good.

One time I was in the VW with my dad, and all of a sudden, a bronco hit us, and my dad's head and mine hit the windshield. It left a place in the glass where our heads hit. It scared me to death. There was a little blood coming from my dad's face, but he was okay, thank god. He had the VW fixed in a shop, but that didn't stop us from having fun. I also remember my mom and me would go down 43 south. There were hills of road, and I would tell her to speed up, and we would go over those hills fast, and our heads would touch the top of the inside of the car. It was so much fun! Her and I had some good times together.

I was very blessed to have such a great place like Bedford to live in and very good parents. When I was a small child, I would stay with the Bowlings family just to have someone to play with. Very blessed all my life. As soon as my feet hit the floor, I thank God for each day of my life. I wear a cross around my neck, and I kiss that cross every morning. What a blessing my God has given me.

Life and times in Bedford has been really good. I remember one time my dad and I and one of the bowling guys were in Roanoke, Virginia. We were playing Puns Boggin. That was when you see a VW, you count the ones that go by, and the one who gets the most wins.

I have also tried to help people out. I am a giver, not a taker. I wish I did have plenty of money so that I could help people out more. I have been blessed, and I have always thought that I should help other people in need. That's the way God would have wanted people to be. I like to meet new people. I love to hear stories about their life. Some are very interested. My mom and dad would always tell me that there would be good and bad days, and they were so right. They were two very wise parents. I just wished I had asked my dad and mom more about life. I'm sure a lot of us think that way.

A lot of people have moved here in the past five to six years. I sure don't blame them. Less crime and also a lot cheaper to live. We have a lot of beauty here in Bedford and a lot of things to do. The weather is good here also. Good people live here in Bedford. Most people drive to Roanoke, Virginia, which is about forty-five minutes away, or they will go to Lynchburg, Virginia, which is about twenty-five minutes away to work each day. They are much bigger places. I remember as a child, we had a nice Christmas parade. I remember one time there were kids pea shooting. That's shooting peas through a straw. One of the guys shot one, and it went inside my ear. Many years later at the hospital, I was getting my ears cleaned. The doctor found the pea inside my ear, thank goodness. He asked me if I was growing a garden in there. My parents and the doctor thought that was funny, and I did too. Like I said, so many good times I have had.

My wife likes to grow flowers and feed the birds. She has hummingbird feeders out, and I am sitting here on my porch watching the hummingbirds. There are four of them, and they fly around and run after each other. I love to fish, but I throw them back. There are a lot of ponds to fish in here. The beauty of the mountains, I remember as a kid going up to the mountains. One time me and the bowling kid, we rode our bicycle all the way to the top of the mountain and back on our ten-speed bike. Lots of fun. They were good times and still are.

As I said, I am just sitting here on the porch listening to the birds and watching the animals. We have lots of wildlife here. If you want to get away from the hustle, Bedford is the place to be. Lots of history here in Virginia. I know there's a big world out there, and lots have gone on in just two years now. I am sixty-four years old and still count my blessings. I'm a very old-soul person. I have a lot of my childhood things my grandmother gave to me. There is a toy that is sixty-one years old, and I wouldn't trade it for the world. She also made me stuffed animal that is also sixty-one years old. I'll always cherish them both.

I remember as a kid playing in Bedford and riding my bike. Bedford is a very safe place to live. I remember going to school as most people still do. We always got out Memorial Day and went back after Labor Day. Today, they go back earlier because of the heat. I remember snow was deep when I was a kid. Lots of good times. Things back then were so much simpler. I sit here thinking of all the good times I have had. Time sure does fly by as you get older.

A lot of good people have gone, but I sure was blessed to have known a lot of them. I talk to my dad's sister a lot. She has helped me a lot. She is ninety years old, but she sure can remember a lot of things that have happened. The last two years in Bedford has gone by fast. I love to play with my grandson. What a joy he is. As a kid, I remember my mom took me to her brother's. We had a horse show, and it was a lot of fun. I got my first guitar at the Body Camp store. My uncle and aunt's granddaughter still lives here. I went by to see her about two years ago.

As I have said, my grandson likes to have fun, and he calls me Papa. I will play all kinds of sports with him. He also likes to play fun games. He has gone to the beach this week, and I miss him a lot. He will be in fifth grade. He starts school August 14. My wife or I will pick him up from school three days a week. He loves to come here and play with us. He's growing up fast. We have kept him on and off since he was born in 2012. He's a blessing for sure.

Had a new home built here in Bedford in 2021. Love it and very blessed living in North Bedford for forty years. I love the mountains. It is beautiful here. Been very busy as you can imagine. Everybody here is so nice. Here I sit on my porch in Bedford, Virginia, at age 64, thinking how blessed I have been. When dad and mom were alive, we would go see my first cousin. We would go to the ice cream shop. Now my cousin is seventy years old. How time flies.

I remember as a kid all the good times in Bedford. Used to go to a place in town called Greens Drug Store. They had a place where you could get something to eat also. Now it is a place for the veterans. My dad was always helping people when they were cold in the winter. My mom would load up to seven to eight people at the armory.

She would take them home after the basketball games. A very sweet person she was.

My wife's mother named the park in Bedford Liberty Lake Park. It was called Liberty in the olden days. I remember when I was small, the lady next door fed the birds, also had them as pets. She was very good with them. She was also a very good cook. I got a meal from her every day. She baked delicious pies. I used to go to milk cows for her and her husband. We would also go to the garden. I used to help them get groceries once a week. His name was Sam Fogle, and a man named Monre Witt lived with them. They were good folks. I would go help them get a list of items because they could not read. They also had a car cover engine in the back of their house. They had a son named Robert who was fifteen years older than me. He was like a brother to me. I loved that guy and his parents. Again, good times in Bedford, Virginia.

I remember when Bedford had a lot of business. Now only two original ones are left in town. Fifty years later, it is still a nice place to live. Not much has changed, just some stores. I am sure there are a lot of good towns out there, but Bedford has got the beauty. Just more people here, probably only about 25 percent of people are from Bedford. Like I said, now that I am older, I love to hang out with my grandson and play and just relax.

I have changed churches. I found out Bowling's grandfather and grandmother live beside the church. Good to know not much has changed here.

Love to go fishing with my friends. The Bowlings also had a lot of family reunions. We also went camping with them. Had a lot of fun. As a kid, I played sports, mostly baseball and basketball. I remember we use to go to Big Island to play baseball. My wife's mother use to be a referee. She loved sports. There was a river near where we played in Big Island. It was a good river to kayak in. To this day, people still take a boat to that river. Water at that river supplies a lot of energy.

I've just seen my old friend, the Bowling guy, the other day. A lot of great memories when we were young. I've been very blessed. My grandson and I had lots of fun yesterday at the neighbor's pool. He's a great kid.

There used to be a yo-yo competition at the minute market in Bedford. I loved that. I used to get ribbons for that. Also in the summer. I went to the YMCA camp. I love that also. I went to a cooking school one summer in Bedford. I loved that also. But I don't do a lot of cooking now. My wife is a great cook. I was also in the Boy Scouts. We went camping a lot, troop 183. I just loved it! I have done all kinds of fun things. I also used to go camping with the Bowlings and Mom and Dad. Growing up was a lot of fun here in Bedford.

I love to go to church here in Bedford on Sundays. We have a nice preacher, Ethan Strickler. He's a good guy and only forty-one years old. Very smart. My friend Randy goes there. He is also a preacher and a judge here in Bedford. He's a really nice guy.

Growing up, I had a clawfoot bathtub. I didn't know what a shower was until I was eighteen years old. I loved that bathtub. All in all, Bedford was a good place. If you ever see your way come to Bedford, Virginia, you will like it here.

There is also a lot of good fishing here. My dad used to tell me this was a good place to live fifty years ago for climate, traffic, and people. If you like to hunt, there is a lot of good hunting here. I would tell anyone to come visit here. You will like it in Bedford, Virginia.

If I ever get well off, I will help a lot of people in need. I try to help people all I can. There is a lot of need here. I'm thankful for the beauty God has given me. He was the start, and he will also be the end. In the last few years, from sixty-two to sixty-four years old, I have seen a lot of good things and a lot of bad things. So many good things I could tell you about Bedford.

Don't get me wrong. Bedford is a nice and beautiful place. I have lived in Bedford all my life except when I was out of town. I lived on the north side of Bedford for forty years. You also have mountain range here where you can also have picnics and family gatherings. If you are able to make it to Bedford, I would say visit the Blue Ridge Mountains and the D-Day Memorial, also Smith Mountain Lake. There is a lot of camping on the mountain. Like I've said, Bedford is a good place. I am still blessed with work. I work part time here. I've been working since fourteen years old. I like to keep myself busy. Got to give it to my God. He has blessed me with good health. The neighbors next door just went down the road. They're both at seventy-six. She has bone cancer, and she has treatments. He is a Vietnam vet. He was in Walter Reed Hospital for a year. He has health issues too. They are good Christian people.

I could keep on and on about Bedford, Virginia. There is so much to tell. Like I said, my grandson is a joy. His dad is a veteran also. He was in the army and in the Iraq War. He has seen a lot also. Doesn't like to talk much about it to this day. I thank God for good people—firefighters, policemen, nurses, doctors, teachers etc. They make this place great. All in all, Bedford has been a lot of fun. I hope to have many good days ahead.

I'm sitting outside as I write this. It's a beautiful day. I'm looking at the mountains and the deer in the backyard. I just saw some does with their babies. Saw a buck also. I was walking the other morning, and I saw a bear. He was about 200 lb. He was walking on the other side of our home. He went across the road and into the woods. The turkeys and their babies are cute to look at. My wife was sitting on the front porch one day, and a bear came close to the porch walking. Scared her.

My grandson and I have a lot of fun. We go down the creek on our four-wheelers. It is a very nice place to retire or visit. If you ever get a chance, come to Bedford. You would like it a lot. It is God's country. A very nice place to settle down with a family. My grandson and I have a 1966 VW. He is now ten and learning to drive a straight drive. He is a very good boy, growing up so fast. I also have a 1963 SS Nova. I plan on giving him that one day. He will be a lucky boy. It's all God's creation, so let him enjoy it all. I love spring time. I have always loved the spring. If I had to do it all over again, I would have taken care of my mom and dad. I lost my job of twenty-five years for her. I love them very much, and I miss them a lot, just like a lot of people do when they lose someone. Hope you can come visit Bedford, Virginia, one day. I think you will like it. Everything I have written is true. Until next time. Thanks.

About the Author

Tim was born in Bedford, Virginia, in 1959. He had very loving and wonderful parents. He was raised in Bedford and lived in an 1849 home. He was very blessed.